New Year, Better Me

Eamon Lindsell

BookLeaf
Publishing

Presentation by *BookLeaf Publishing*

Web: www.bookleafpub.com

E-mail: info@bookleafpub.com

ISBN: 9789357441377

First edition 2023

Dawn

The Sun Rose.

New Year, Better Me

New year
New me
Same fears
Same glee

Same world
Same struggles
Unfurled
But still troubled

Same plight
Same suffering
New fight
And hope of recovering

New outlook
New objective

The ground shook
With a new perspective

New motivation
New disposition
New determination
And giving myself permission
To love and to be loved
To hold and to behold
My world as it is now… in my control

So I step in with vigour
And new energy
To this significant new year
As a much better Me

How Many Times?

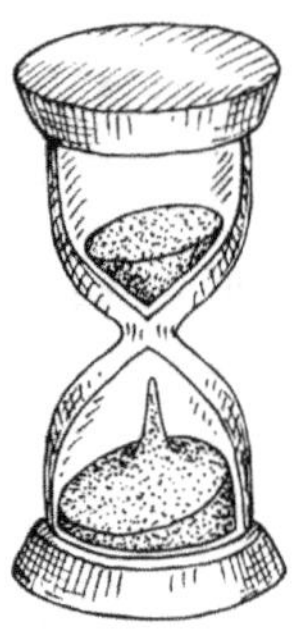

How many times can you start again
They say if you get knocked down 9 times, then
get up 10
But getting up is harder than it sounds
When your whole body feels like it's stuck to the
ground
Like you're being held or being pushed back
But you're really trying hard and you don't want
to crack,
Under the pressure of it all
The best thing to do? Call
For help is out there
Whether you know it or not
There are people who care
Some a little, most a lot
It could be friends, it could be family

It could be professionals, but all of them can be
There when you need them, to pull you up
To help you stand, to fill your cup
To give you support
And unlock your strength
So you don't resort to extremes
Or go to great lengths to scream for help
Is out there
So seek it, don't reject it
You're not weak if you don't accept it
You'll have a chance at relief
And become powerful beyond belief
So how many times can you start again
As many as it takes until you find your Zen

Day

It's Light Shone.

I Just Took It

I was pushed
I was punched
In a bush
And at lunch

I was teased
I was taunted
With ease
I was haunted

I just sighed
And I smiled
Never cried
Never riled

I just took
Never told

I wasn't shook
Didn't fold

I was gracious
I was good
Not ostentatious
No one understood

But that is how it had to be…

United Once Again

The joy, the passion, the despair
You're responsible for the greying and thinning
of my hair

The pride, the setback, the fight
It's been years of lows after generations at great
height

The desire, the prospect, the hope
If it's another false dawn, I don't think I could
cope

The inconsistency, the anxiety, the belief
Hearing the final whistle and feeling relief

I'm optimistic, I'm expecting, I'm excited
Because it finally feels like we've got back our
Manchester United

On A Cold And Frosty Morning

Morning Breeze
Below zero degrees
My fingers freeze
And there's pain in my knees
A sense of unease
A noise in the trees
I think this could be me!
My body seized
I can't breathe
I shout "no, please"
But then…
I feel relieved
Realising my senses were deceived
By a small woodland creature who by my
presence, was aggrieved

The Grey

12

Clouds Appeared.

Where Are We Now?

What a world we live in
It's hard to explain
What life is like
In just one refrain

Our tech is the best
But also the worst
Sometimes we feel blessed
Sometimes we feel cursed

For some, we have the world in the palm of our
hand
More than we could ever need yet still harm our
land

We burn, we pollute, we cause global warming
How much must be destroyed before we heed
the warning

Abundance of music and film, the golden age of
TV
We're distracted by drama, by money, by
celebrity

But I have hope that all this can change
That we're able to stop the hate and disdain

That is the only way we'll continue…

Where Are We Going?

Who knows
Where the wind will blow
At any given moment

But what is clear
When it comes to ideas
You need to disclose
If you oppose
Or if you're a proponent

Optimism is key
To the future of you and me
We must be positive
It is duty, not prerogative
To safeguard the future
With wit and good humour
To baffle and flummox any opponent

Darkness

The Light Has Gone.

Good or Bad?

Is it good or bad
This thing we have
That we hold so tight in the palm of our hands

It takes up so much of our time and attention
Checking for a tag, or a post, or a mention
Connecting us with loved ones and staying in
touch
Finding a game and playing too much

Checking the news or the sports results
Googling things we should know as adults

Booking the cinema or a trip to go bowling
Then checking your socials and before you
know it, doom scrolling

Watching video after video, seeing post after
post
Becoming so engrossed
It's like an addiction, undiagnosed

It's impossible to live without
in this modern day
A place full of facts and doubt
That can grow your mind or make it decay

Enabling you to work from wherever you can
Or sending the documents you need to scan
It can capture every moment so you don't forget
But you're sold to by corporations' who want
you in debt

So is it good or bad? It's hard to tell
But stay in control, or it can become a deep dark
hell

Dry January

Frosty morning
Weather warning
Bed is calling
Whilst I'm yawning
But…

Work is needed
To keep the house heated
So I remained seated
With my motivation depleted
But…

We keep on plodding
Using coffee to stop nodding
For spring will come knocking
And we'll all be hopping
Soon…

The sun will shine
The cold weather behind
The days will be fine
And we'll be drinking wine

You Are There

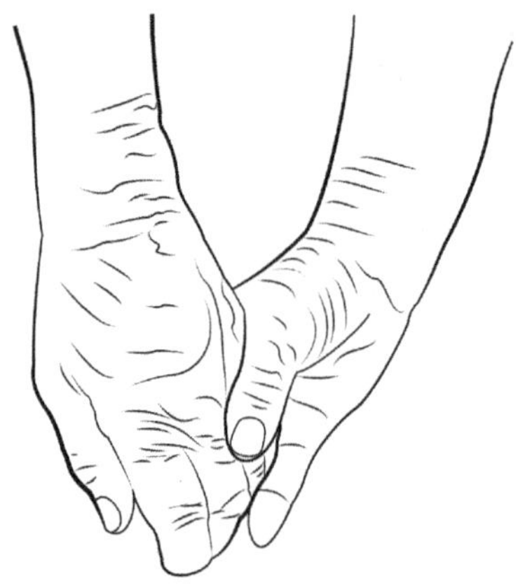

Whatever we need
You are there
Love and support
You are there
Good times and bad times
You are there

Whenever we bleed
You are there
Always, in short
You are there
When the final bell chimes
You'll be there

New Light

23

Dawn Grows.

The Best Of Us Both

You got the best of us both
And more besides, with room for growth
The infectious laugh
The stubborn shout
You don't do things by half
There is no doubt
That you are of us

You got the best of us both
And more besides, with room for growth
The strongest of wills

As brave as they come
You walk in, the room stills
To your charm, all succumb
Its clear, that you are of us

You got the best of us both
And more besides, with room for growth
The kindest soul
Wise beyond your years
You make us whole
And bring us to tears
With your happiness and joy
Confident never coy
Yes, you are of us

You Be You

I want to run
I want to play
I want to have fun
All through the day

I want to craft
I want to paint
I want to laugh
Until I faint

I want to draw
I want to jump
I want to explore
Until I'm tired and slump

I want to read stories
I want to play make believe
I want to be sporty
Splash in puddles and kick leaves

I want to be bold
I want to be free
But I can't cause I'm old
And have responsibilities

But you can
And you do
Every chance that you get
So here I am
To support you
So you never have to fret

New Day

A New Day Begins.

I Can Be Me

I'm writing these words
In order to be heard
For the first time in my life

For so much is hidden
Emotions were forbidden
And you can't show struggle or strife

That was the mantra, imposed, if unspoken
Show no weakness, stay closed and unbroken

Joy was a luxury I could not afford
Pain was something to be ignored
As was I
Especially if I cried

There was no time for sadness
No room for anger
No stability or support, no sign of an anchor

At least not for me
But those around were free to feel
Whatever they want, or need to heal
They could be heard
Without being considered a burden

But things have changed, I have love, I have
safety
I can be Me, freely and safely

So now is the time to show my true self
Without shadow or stealth
I'm hoping to finally achieve good emotional
health